Publishing Director: Michael Skrigitil
Editor: Carolyn Pytlyk
Sound Director: Elena Rumyantseva
Book Illustrator: Natalia Gavrilova
Book Designer: Elena Pushkina
Actors and Announcers:

Maria Dodenkova
Lyubov Litova
Natalia Nikitina
Aleksei Leonov
Denis Garmash
Evgeniy Rozhko

Sputnik Workbook: An Introductory Russian Language Course, Part I
ISBN: 978-0-9939139-1-4

Copyright © 2014 by TLTNetwork Inc.
Victoria, BC, Canada

ТЕМА 1.
Буквы и звуки

Урок 1

Russians write in cursive. If you receive a handwritten note in Russian, it will be in cursive. Your Russian teacher will write on the board in cursive. Russian print and cursive letters are quite different. You need to learn both and this workbook will help you master your cursive writing.

 Упражне́ние 1.1.   Practice writing letters.

А а — *А а*   О о — *О о*   Э э — *Э э*   У у — *У у*

М м — *М м*   П п — *П п*   Б б — *Б б*

Н н — *Н н*   Т т — *Т т*   Д д — *Д д*

А _____   *а* _____

М _____   *м* _____

ма _____ *ам* _____   *мама* _____

П _____   *п* _____

па _____ *ап* _____   *папа* _____

Д _____   *д* _____

до _____ *дом* _____   *дома* _____

Мама дома _____

Э _____ *э* _____   *О* _____ *о* _____

Т _____ *т* _____   *Это Тома* _____

У _____ *у* _____ *ум* _____   *Тут* _____

Б _____ *б* _____ *Ба* _____   *бу* _____

Н _____ *н* _____ *на* _____   *банан* _____

Это дом, а это дома́.

_____

Вот фонтан. Там вода.

_____

Do not confuse the letters *М м* and *Т т*.

м _____   *т* _____

Мама _____   *Том* _____   *атом* _____

📖 **Упражне́ние 1.2.**   Practice writing new letters.

Cc — *Cc*   Зз — *Зз*   Вв — *Вв*   Фф — *Фф*

Кк — *Кк*   Гг — *Гг*   Хх — *Хх*

$\mathcal{C}$ _____ с _____ З _____ з _____

$\mathcal{B}$ _____ в _____ Ф _____ ф _____

$\mathcal{C}о$ _____ са _____ ос _____ оса _____

$За$ _____ зо _____ аз _____ ваза _____

$Вот$ _____ ву _____ Фа _____ фо _____

> Do not confuse the capital **З** with **Э**. The letter **З з** looks like number 3, whereas **Э э** is a semicircle with a line in the middle.

$Э$ _____ З _____ Э _____ З _____

$Это\ ваза.$ _____ Звук з. _____.

X _____ х _____ ох _____ ух _____

Xa _____ ухо _____ эхо _____ уха _____

$Ж$ _____ к _____ Г _____ г _____

$Жа$ _____ ко _____ ук _____ звук _____

📖✎ **Упражнéние 1.3.** Practice writing simple phrases.

$Как\ вас\ зовут? - Антон.$ _____

$Кто\ там? - Папа.$ _____

Тут сова, а там оса. _____

Это кот, а это собака. _____

 Упражнéние 1.4. You are making flash cards for a friend who is learning Russian (or may be for yourself). Describe the objects in each picture to memorise the words. Use various structures like: Это дом. *This is a house.* Тут пáпа. *Here is dad.* Там мáма. *There is mom.* А вот Антóн. *And here is Anton.*

_____   _____   _____

_____   _____   _____

Тут — *here*   Там — *over there*

_____

Here is a fountain and the house is over there.

Урок 2

📖✒ **Упражнéние 1.5.** Practice writing Russian cursive.

Л л — *Лл*   Р р — *Рр*   И и — *Ии*   ы — *ы*
Ж ж — *Жж*   Ш ш — *Шш*   Щ щ — *Щщ*   Ч ч — *Чч*

л _____ *л* _____ *Р* _____ *р* _____

Ла _____ *лам* _____ *лампа* _____

Лл and *Мм* have **front hooks**

Ро _____ *ру* _____ *рука* _____

И _____ *и* _____ *ы* _____

Или _____ *ли* _____ *мы* _____ *ты* _____

Вот рис, рыба и сыр. _____

Мы за мир. _____

Ж _____ *ж* _____ *Ш* _____ *ш* _____

Жа _____ *жу* _____ *журнал* _____

Шо _____ *ша* _____ *шарф* _____

Щ _____ *щ* _____ *Ч* _____ *ч* _____

Щу _____ *щи* _____ *овощи* _____

Ча _____ *чк* _____ *ручка* _____

Это нужно. _____

Это важно. _____

Можно карандаш? _____

У нас на ужин борщ. _____

Упражнéние 1.6. Sort the words о́вощи, суп, ша́пка, врач, плащ, лимо́н, ры́ба, са́хар, шо́рты, су́ши, ру́чка into edible and inedible. Write them in cursive.

Edible

_____

_____

_____

_____

_____

_____

Inedible

_____

_____

_____

_____

_____

_____

Урок 3

✏ **Упражнёние 1.7.** Practice writing Russian cursive.

> *Я я* has **front hook** like *Л л* and *М м*

Ц ц — *Ц ц*   Й й — *Й й*

Е е — *Е е*   Ё ё — *Ё ё*   Ю ю — *Ю ю*   Я я — *Я я*

Ц _____ *ц* _____ *Й* _____ *й* _____

Ца _____ *ци* _____ *цифра* _____

й _____ *ой* _____ *ай* _____ *ий* _____

> Do not confuse the letter **й** with **и**. The letter й appears after a vowel: **мой**, **чай** and usually does not begin a word (loan words like **йо́гурт** are rare exceptions). The "hat" on top of **й** is required.

Цирк _____ *мой* _____ *чай* _____

Это чайник и чашка. _____

Е _____ *е* _____ *Ё* _____ *ё* _____

Ю _____ *ю* _____ *Я* _____ *я* _____

ля _____ *ял* _____ *мя* _____ *ям* _____

Ел _____ *ёлка* _____ *моё* _____ *твоё* _____

Юл _____ *Юлия* _____ *Яна* _____ *Зоя* _____

Упражне́ние 1.8.   Sort the nouns by grammatical gender.

звук, ма́сло, журна́л, бу́ква, сло́во, бана́н, молоко́, ру́чка, чай, у́лица, столи́ца, у́жин

он	она́	оно́
звук	*буква*	*масло*

 Упражне́ние 1.9.   Describe the items in the drawings as 'my'. Remember to change 'my' for gender.

Образец: *Это* <u>*моя машина*</u> .

Это _____

Это _____

Это _____

и _____

Это _____

Урок 4

📖✏️ **Упражне́ние 1.10.** Practice writing Russian cursive.

ь — *ь*   ъ — *ъ*

> The letters **ь** and **ъ** never begin a word. These letters always appear after a consonant.

ь _____ *ть* _____ *ль* _____ *нь* _____

апельсин _____ *быть* _____ *жизнь* _____

ъ _____ *съ* _____ *дъ* _____ *нь* _____

съел _____ *объект* _____

Зоя съела апельсин. _____
Zoya has eaten an orange.

Игорь съел яблоко. _____
Igor has eaten an apple.

📖✏️ **Упражне́ние 1.11.** Write in cursive what fruit you have already eaten today: апельси́н, бана́н, лимо́н, or я́блоко. If you have not eaten any of your daily fruit servings yet, write it. Simply add **не** in front of the verb to negate the action: Я не съел... (*for a guy*) or Я не съела... (*for a girl*).

_____

_____

Упражнéние 1.12. Write a note that will introduce you to your classmates. Follow the model below, replacing the words in bold with information about yourself.

Привет! Меня зовут Зоя. Я студентка. Я из России.

_____

_____

_____

Урок 5

Упражне́ние 1.13. Read the questions and write down the answers. Follow the model.

— *Это кофе?*

— *Нет, это не кофе, это сок.*

— *Это мёд?*

— _____

— *Это машина?*

— _____

— *Это апельсин?*

— _____

— *Это журнал?*

— _____

Упражнéние 1.14. Look at the image and list all these breakfast foods in Russian. Write in cursive.

Завтрак

Каша, _____

_____

_____

_____

Упражнéние 1.15. **Ну́жно встрéтиться!** Write a short note to your Russian friend. In this note:

- greet your friend;
- say that you need to meet;
- say when (утром, днём, вечером) and at what time;
- say that you'll be at home and invite your friend to come over;
- say "Bye";
- write your name at the end.

You don't know much Russian grammar yet, but you can say all this anyway!
Use phrases introduced in exercise 1.5-14 in your textbook as construction blocks for your note.

Алфавит.
Notes on Cursive Writing

Буква Letter	Прописью In cursive	Звук Sound similar to
А а	*А а*	**ar** in f**ar**
Б б	*Б б*	**b** in **b**ox
В в	*В в*	**v** in **v**oice
Г г	*Г г*	**g** in **g**o
Д д	*Д д*	**d** in **d**ay
Е е	*Е е*	**ye** in **ye**llow or **e** in **e**xit
Ё ё	*Ё ё*	**yo** in **yo**ghurt
Ж ж	*Ж ж*	**s** in plea**s**ure
З з	*З з*	**z** in **z**oo
И и	*И и*	**ee** in ch**ee**se
Й й	*Й й*	**y** in bo**y**
К к	*К к*	**k** in **k**ey
Л л	*Л л*	**l** in **l**amp
М м	*М м*	**m** in **m**an
Н н	*Н н*	**n** in **n**ote
О о	*О о*	**o** in n**o**t
П п	*П п*	**p** in **p**et

Буква Letter	Прописью In cursive	Звук Sound similar to
Р р	*Р р*	**r** in **r**ock (but rolled)
С с	*С с*	**s** in **s**un
Т т	*Т т*	**t** in **t**ea
У у	*У у*	**oo** in m**oo**n
Ф ф	*Ф ф*	**f** in **f**ood
Х х	*Х х*	**ch** in Scottish lo**ch**
Ц ц	*Ц ц*	**ts** in ca**ts**
Ч ч	*Ч ч*	**ch** in **ch**at
Ш ш	*Ш ш*	**sh** in **sh**ort
Щ щ	*Щ щ*	**shch** in fre**sh ch**eese
ъ	*ъ*	no sound
ы	*ы*	**i** in **i**ll
ь	*ь*	no sound
Э э	*Э э*	**e** in **e**nd
Ю ю	*Ю ю*	like **u** in **u**se
Я я	*Я я*	like **ya** in **ya**rd

- The letters *л*, *м*, *я* have front hooks: или, моя, мама.

- Do not confuse *м* with *т* or *З* with *Э*: *Это моя мама. Это Зоя и Зина.*

- The letter *ш* terminates on the base line and connects with another letter at the bottom. Avoid writing the English *w* instead of the *ш*: *машина.*

- Soft sign (мягкий знак) looks like a *small* number six: *ь*. Do not write it as an English "b". Hard sign is also small but with a tail on top: *ъ*. The letter *ы* looks like the soft sign with an extra line.

- The lower case *у*, *д*, *з* have a long tail, whereas *ц* and *щ* have very short tails.

- The letter **г** has two rounded corners: *г*. The letter **ч** has a sharp top corner and a rounded bottom: *ч*.

- *д* and *в* are the only *tall* lower-case letters.

Упражнéние 1.16. Review handwritten Russian letters. Write each letter at least three times.

А _____   *а* _____

Б _____   *б* _____

В _____   *в* _____

Г _____   *г* _____

Д _____   *д* _____

Е _____   *е* _____

Ё _____   *ё* _____

Ж _____   *ж* _____

З _____   *з* _____

И _____   *и* _____

Й _____   *й* _____

К _____   *к* _____

Л _____   *л* _____

$\mathcal{M}$ ———————————————————— *м* ————————————————————

$\mathcal{H}$ ———————————————————— *н* ————————————————————

$\mathcal{O}$ ———————————————————— *о* ————————————————————

$\mathcal{\Pi}$ ———————————————————— *п* ————————————————————

$\mathcal{P}$ ———————————————————— *р* ————————————————————

$\mathcal{C}$ ———————————————————— *с* ————————————————————

$\mathcal{T}$ ———————————————————— *т* ————————————————————

$\mathcal{У}$ ———————————————————— *у* ————————————————————

$\mathcal{Ф}$ ———————————————————— *ф* ————————————————————

$\mathcal{X}$ ———————————————————— *х* ————————————————————

$\mathcal{Ц}$ ———————————————————— *ц* ————————————————————

$\mathcal{Ч}$ ———————————————————— *ч* ————————————————————

$\mathcal{Ш}$ ———————————————————— *ш* ————————————————————

$\mathcal{Щ}$ ———————————————————— *щ* ————————————————————

$\mathcal{Ч}$ ———————————————————— *ч* ————————————————————

ъ ———————————————————— *ы* ————————————————————

ь ————————————————————

$\mathcal{Э}$ ———————————————————— *э* ————————————————————

$\mathcal{Ю}$ ———————————————————— *ю* ————————————————————

$\mathcal{Я}$ ———————————————————— *я* ————————————————————

ТЕМА 2.
Кто вы? Откуда вы?

 Упражнéние 2.1. **Как их зовýт? Кто онú? Откýда онú?** An international group of tourists arrived in Moscow. You are the group leader trying to remember each person's name, profession, and what country he/she is from. Write their identification cards. Follow the model. *Make up their identities.*

Маша. Студентка из России.

> **их** — *their*
> **они́** — *they*

_____

_____

_____

_____

_____

_____

You:	_____

 Упражне́ние 2.2. **Grammatical gender of nouns.** Your friend missed a Russian class where you learned about grammatical gender of nouns. Sort the nouns below by their gender and explain the concept to your friend.

A) Regular: журна́л, уче́бник, кни́га, письмо́, уро́к, сло́во, статья́, диало́г, упражне́ние, страни́ца, исто́рия, пра́вило, вопро́с, отве́т.

	Masculine	Feminine	Neuter
Ending			

Б) Masculine or feminine? Explain to your friend what endings can be misleading and how to figure out the gender of the following nouns: па́па, тетра́дь, слова́рь, де́душка, ба́бушка, ночь, жизнь, дочь, календа́рь, любо́вь, дя́дя, тётя, Ма́ша, Ди́ма. Sort them into masculine and feminine.

Masculine (он)	
Feminine (она́)	

 Упражне́ние 2.3. **Verb. Present tense.** Create your own chart of verb conjugation patterns. Use the verb **знать** — *to know* for the 1st conjugation and **по́мнить** — *to remember* for the 2nd conjugation.

Personal Pronoun	1st conjugation *знать*	2nd conjugation *по́мнить*
я		
ты		
он, она, кто		
мы		
вы		
они		

Before adding endings
- remove two final letters (-**ть**) from the infinitive if it's a 1st conjugation verb
- remove three final letters (-**ить**) from the infinitive if it's a 2nd conjugation verb

Упражнéние 2.4. **Verb. Present tense.** **A)** You are working for a tourist agency in Moscow organising bus tours. Tourists from different countries are going on a tour around Moscow, but they need a translator as their Russian is limited. These people were asked to comment on their language skills. Based on the information provided in the chart, write a brief report for your boss describing what languages they speak and understand. Follow the model that begins your report.

	по-рýсски	по-англи́йски	по-немéцки	по-францýзски	по-япóнски	по-испáнски
Си́монас, Литвá						
говори́т	свобóдно	хорошó	—	—	—	—
понимáет	свобóдно	хорошó	немнóго	—	—	—
Мóника, Испáния						
говори́т	немнóго	плóхо	—	—	—	свобóдно
понимáет	немнóго	плóхо	—	—	—	свобóдно
Пáтрик, Фрáнция						
говори́т	немнóго	хорошó	—	свобóдно	—	—
понимáет	немнóго	хорошó	—	свобóдно	—	—
Карл, Гермáния						
говори́т	плóхо	хорошó	свобóдно	—	—	—
понимáет	плóхо	хорошó	свобóдно	—	—	немнóго
Сáра, США						
говори́т	немнóго	свобóдно	—	—	—	хорошó
понимáет	немнóго	свобóдно	—	—	—	хорошó

Группа 1. Москва

Симонас из Литвы свободно говорит и понимает по-русски, хорошо говорит и понимает по-английски, немного понимает по-немецки.

Б) Now you need to choose an interpreter for the group. Read what Russian translators' write in their professional profiles about their language skills and write out the name of <u>one person</u> who you think can work with <u>all tourists in this group</u>. Fill in a brief recommendation form below (рекоменда́ция) specifying what languages this interpreter speaks and understands.

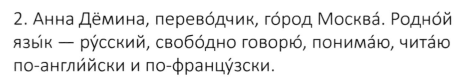

1. Анто́н Харла́мов, перево́дчик, го́род Москва́. Родно́й язы́к- ру́сский, свобо́дно говорю́, понима́ю, чита́ю по-англи́йски и по-неме́цки.

2. Анна Дёмина, перево́дчик, го́род Москва́. Родно́й язы́к — ру́сский, свобо́дно говорю́, понима́ю, чита́ю по-англи́йски и по-францу́зски.

3. Никола́й Воро́нин, перево́дчик, го́род Москва́. Родно́й язы́к — ру́сский, свобо́дно говорю́, понима́ю и чита́ю по-япо́нски, немно́го понима́ю по-францу́зски и по-англи́йски.

4. Татья́на Соро́кина, перево́дчик, го́род Москва́. Родно́й язы́к — ру́сский, свобо́дно говорю́, понима́ю, чита́ю по-япо́нски и по-францу́зски.

5. Светла́на Петро́ва, перево́дчик, го́род Москва́. Родно́й язы́к — ру́сский, свобо́дно говорю́, понима́ю, чита́ю по-англи́йски и по-испа́нски, немно́го говорю́ и понима́ю по-францу́зски.

Рекомендация

Имя и фамилия

_____

Комментарий

_____

_____

_____

_____

Упражне́ние 2.5. **Verb. Present tense.** Your boss in a tourist agency in Moscow asked you to comment on your language skills. Write a summary of what language(s) you speak, understand, can read and how well. Use adverbs like хорошо́, пло́хо, бы́стро, ме́дленно, пра́вильно, свобо́дно to describe your skills.

Имя и фамилия

_____

Языки

_____

_____

_____

_____

Упражнéние 2.6. **Verb. Past tense.** Imagine you have a diary where you write about your Russian experiences. Yesterday you and your friend Thomas went to the house where your Russian friend Masha lives with her family. Masha helped you and Thomas with Russian homework. In your diary entry you should:

- mention each person in the house (мáма, пáпа, etc.);
- using the past tense of verbs читáть, рабóтать, игрáть, дéлать (урóки), describe what people in that house were doing;
- at the end, say that you and your friends (Мáша, Тóмас и я) were speaking Russian;
- write short simple statements (like in the model below) staying within the limits of grammar and structure familiar to you.

Образéц: *Мама читала журнал.*

Что делали Маша, её мама, папа и брат вчера вечером

_____

_____

_____

_____

_____

_____

_____

_____

Повторя́ем. Chapter 2 Review

 Упражне́ние 2.7. **Что мы изуча́ли и что мы тепе́рь зна́ем.** Write a summary of what you have learned in chapter 2. Here is what you should mention:

Часть 1

- what you did in class (reading, speaking, etc.);
- what you know now about some characters introduced in this chapter (pick two or three);
- what Russian words for professions you have learned (list four-six words as examples);

Часть 2

- what Russian words are difficult to read (list four-six words);
- what Russian words you don't remember well (list four-six words);
- what Russian words are easy to read (list three words).

Refer to the text **Что мы изуча́ли** in Уро́к 6 (Те́ма 2) in your textbook if necessary but do not copy it. Use the text from Уро́к 6 as a model to create your own.

Что мы изучали и что мы теперь знаем

Тема 2

Часть 1. _____

_____

_____

_____

_____

_____

_____

_____

_____

_____

Часть 2. _____

_____

_____

_____

_____

_____

_____

_____

_____

_____

ТЕМА 3.
Како́й вы челове́к? Что вы лю́бите?

 Упражне́ние 3.1. **Како́й он? Кака́я она?** As a group leader of international tourists you have been observing these people for a few days and now are making notes about their personalities. Use two-three adjectives from the list that describe them best. Refer to Упражне́ние 2.1 to review their names and occupations. Continue making up their identities. Comment on your own personality at the end.

Suggested adjectives: до́брый, весёлый, у́мный, краси́вый, интере́сный, ску́чный, хоро́ший, тала́нтливый, серьёзный, смешно́й.

Образе́ц:

Маша весёлая и умная.
Она хорошая студентка.

_____

_____

_____

_____

You:

_____

_____

Упражнéние 3.2. **Рýсский или росси́йский?** Complete the word combinations with the correct term for Russian (refer to Урóк 1 of Тéма 3 in your textbook to learn about the difference between рýсский and росси́йский). Change the adjectives endings to feminine where necessary.

Образéц: 1. *росси́йский флаг*

2. _____ *литература*

3. _____ *сказка*

4. _____ *паспорт*

5. _____ *конституция*

6. _____ *баня*

7. _____ *язык*

8. _____ *словарь*

9. _____ *парламент*

Can you tell the meaning of these international words without looking them up in the dictionary?

литератýра —

пáспорт —

конститýция —

парлáмент —

Упражнéние 3.3. **Plural of nouns. Regular forms.** Change the following nouns into plural. Mark the noun's gender (m., f., n.) before you choose the ending. Is the ending hard or soft?

Образéц: *маши́на* (*f., hard*) — *маши́ны*

вопрóс (____) _____   *словáрь* (____) _____

отвéт (____) _____   *тетрáдь* (____) _____

рабóта (____) _____   *статья́* (____) _____

прáвило (____) _____   *газéта* (____) _____

журнáл (____) _____   *упражнéние* (____) _____

Упражне́ние 3.4. **Plural of nouns. The 7-letter spelling rule.** Write the following nouns in the plural. Check all nouns that are subject to the 7-letter rule.

Singular	Plural	7-letter rule
ру́чка	ру́чки	✓
каранда́ш	_____	☐
студе́нт	_____	☐
студе́нтка	_____	☐
диало́г	_____	☐
врач	_____	☐
гита́ра	_____	☐
бизнесме́н	_____	☐
перево́дчик	_____	☐
перево́д	_____	☐
гара́ж	_____	☐
магази́н	_____	☐
предложе́ние	_____	☐
това́рищ	_____	☐

Упражнёние 3.5. **Plural of nouns. Exceptions.** Write the following nouns in the plural. Here you have different kinds of irregular plurals. Check the type of a noun's irregularity.

Singular	Plural	No change in the plural	Masculine with -á/-я in the plural	Different stem in the plural
па́спорт	паспорта́	☐	✓	☐
пальто́	_____	☐	☐	☐
метро́	_____	☐	☐	☐
профе́ссор	_____	☐	☐	☐
учи́тель	_____	☐	☐	☐
челове́к	_____	☐	☐	☐
ра́дио	_____	☐	☐	☐
дом	_____	☐	☐	☐
го́род	_____	☐	☐	☐
друг	_____	☐	☐	☐
такси́	_____	☐	☐	☐
пиани́но	_____	☐	☐	☐
ко́фе	_____	☐	☐	☐

Упражнéние 3.6. **Adjective agreement.** Write down word combinations. Remember to change adjective endings to make them agree with the noun in gender and number. Keep in mind 5-letter and 7-letter spelling rules. This simple drill will help you get used to changing adjective endings.

Образéц: 1. краси́вый — го́род, у́лица, зда́ние, лю́ди

краси́вый го́род, краси́вая у́лица, краси́вое зда́ние, краси́вые лю́ди

2. интере́сный — расска́з, ска́зка, сло́во, но́вости

_____

_____

3. тру́дный — перево́д, статья́, упражне́ние, слова́

_____

_____

4. просто́й — диало́г, грамма́тика, предложе́ние, те́ксты

_____

_____

5. ма́ленький — дом, кварти́ра, окно́, маши́ны

_____

_____

6. хоро́ший — студе́нт, гита́ра, упражне́ние, лю́ди

_____

_____

Упражнѐние 3.7.   Adjective or adverb? These phrases are very helpful for describing people and their different skills. Translate the words in parentheses to complete the phrases.

1.   Тóмас *хорошо́* (*good, well*) читáет по-рýсски. Он _____
_____ (*cheerful*) человéк
и _____ (*talented*) музыкáнт. Тóмас из Канáды.

2.   Юми _____ (*smart*) _____ (*serious*)
студéнтка из Япóнии. Она óчень _____ (*beautifully*)
поёт. Юми _____ (*not bad*) говори́т по-рýсски.

3.   Мáша — студéнтка из Рóссии. Онá óчень _____
_____ (*good, well*) студéнтка. Мáша
_____ (*kind*) и _____ (*cheerful*).

4.   Карл — бизнесмéн из Гермáнии. Он _____ (*serious*)
человéк и _____ (*good, well*) бизнесмéн. Он всё
дéлает _____ (*fast*).

всё — *everything*

Упражнѐние 3.8.   In part A) describe yourself and some of your skills (what you do well, poorly, etc.). In part Б) describe your friend and some of his/her skills. Create sentences similar to the exercise above. Use at least two adjectives and two adverbs in each description.

А) *Я* _____

_____

_____

_____

_____

Б) *Мой друг / Моя подруга* _____

_____

_____

_____

_____

📖✏️ **Упражнéние 3.9.** You friend asks you to explain the difference between nominative and accusative cases. Fill out the chart below with a brief explanation of how each case is used and provide examples. Draw your friend's attention to what endings change and how.

Nominative case use	Examples
_____	_____
_____	_____
_____	_____
_____	_____

Accusative case use	Examples
_____	_____
_____	_____
_____	_____
_____	_____

✏️ **Упражнёние 3.10.**   **Nominative or Accusative?** Read the passage and indicate in the blank whether the noun is in the nominative (N), or accusative (A) case.

Это Мáша (_____). Мáша (_____) — студéнтка(_____) из Росси́и. Онá лю́бит чита́ть и слу́шать му́зыку (_____). Онá чита́ет журна́лы (_____) и кни́ги (_____).

Неда́вно Мáша (_____) чита́ла но́вый англи́йский рома́н (_____), а сейча́с онá чита́ет интере́сную ру́сскую кни́гу (_____). А ещё Мáша (_____) лю́бит слу́шать Земфи́ру (_____). Земфи́ра (_____) — её люби́мая певи́ца (_____).

> её — *her*

✏️ **Упражнёние 3.11.**   **Что вы изуча́ете?** Your boss in the tourist agency wants to know your academic background. Write a note telling:

- what courses you took: Я изуча́л(а)…;
- what courses you are taking now: Я изуча́ю…;
- what your favorite subjects are. Я люблю́… .

Write complete grammatically correct sentences like this one:

Я изуча́л(а) ру́сскую литерату́ру и лингви́стику.

_____

_____

_____

_____

Упражнёние 3.12. All students in Russian language summer school fill out a brief questionnaire on arrival. Not all students coming to the school speak English, but they all have a reading knowledge of Russian. Translate this questionnaire into Russian for them.

Questionnaire

1. What is your name?

2. Where are you from?

3. What do you study?

4. How do you read in Russian?

    * fast

    * slowly

    * very slowly

5. How do you speak Russian?

    * fluently

    * well

    * a little bit

    * very poorly

Анкёта

1. _____

2. _____

3. _____

4. _____

    * _____

    * _____

    * _____

5. _____

    * _____

    * _____

    * _____

    * _____

6. What languages do you know?

6. _____

- English

    - _____

- French

    - _____

- German

    - _____

- Japanese

    - _____

- Spanish

    - _____

- Other languages. What kind?

    - _____

Languages are not capitalised in Russian.

other (adj.) — другóй, другáя, другóе, другúе

7. What do you like to eat and drink?

7. _____

8. What books do you like to read?

8. _____

Повторя́ем. Chapter 3 Review

 Упражне́ние 3.13. **Что мы изуча́ли и что мы тепе́рь зна́ем.** In your Russian diary make a new entry summarising what you learned from chapter 3. Here is what you should mention:

Часть 1.

- what the topic was and what you did in class (learning, reading, speaking, etc.);
- what new adjectives you learned (list four-six);
- what verbs you learned and practiced;
- what new things you learned about our characters Masha, Thomas, and Yumi;

Часть 2.

- what new Russian words from this chapter are difficult to read (list four-six words);
- what new Russian words you do not remember well (list four-six words);
- what new Russian words you think are easy to read and remember (list three words).

You can refer to the text **Что мы изуча́ли** in Уро́к 7 (Те́ма 2) in your textbook, but do not simply copy it. Use the text in Уро́к 7 as a model to create your own.

Что мы изуча́ли и что мы тепе́рь зна́ем

Те́ма 3

Часть 1. _____

_____

_____

_____

_____

_____

_____

_____

Часть 2. _____

_____

ТЕМА 4.
Где вы живёте, у́читесь и рабо́таете?

Упражне́ние 4.1. **Где мы побыва́ли.** With an international group of tourists you visited (побыва́ли) many interesting places last week. Refer to the list of places below and write down one sentence summarising all your visits. Remember to use the preposition в and the prepositional case endings for places.

> неда́вно — *recently*
> побыва́ть (где) — *to visit*

Неда́вно мы побыва́ли _____

_____

_____

_____

Places of interest: Истори́ческий музе́й, Большо́й теа́тр, Моско́вский Кремль, Моско́вское метро́, Моско́вская Консервато́рия.

Упражне́ние 4.2. **Где я хочу́ побыва́ть.**

A) Below is a list of interesting sites to visit in various places. Write a sentence mentioning <u>four places and sites</u> you would like to visit. Use commas to separate your sites in one long sentence.

Образе́ц: Москва́, Истори́ческий музе́й

Я хочу́ побыва́ть в Москве́ в Истори́ческом музе́е, ...

_____

_____

_____

_____

_____

_____

Places of interest: Москва́, Большо́й теа́тр; Санкт-Петербу́рг, Эрмита́ж; Пари́ж, Лувр; Ло́ндон, Брита́нский музе́й; Калифо́рния, Диснейле́нд; Лас-Ве́гас, казино́.

Б) Write one more sentence with personalised information about where you would like to go. Use the internet to find out the correct Russian spelling for two-three sites and places of your choice. Start your sentence this way: *I also want to visit...* **А ещё я хочу́ побыва́ть...** Write in cursive and remember to use the correct preposition and prepositional case endings.

_____

_____

 Упражне́ние 4.3. **Где они́ живу́т, у́чатся, рабо́тают?** Write a short description for each person below telling where they are from, where they live, their profession, where they work and study.

Образе́ц: Ма́ша, Росси́я, Москва́, гид-перево́дчик, турфи́рма, студе́нтка, университе́т, лингвисти́ческий факульте́т

Ма́ша из Росси́и. Она́ живёт в Москве́. По профе́ссии Ма́ша гид-перево́дчик, рабо́тает в турфи́рме. А ещё Ма́ша студе́нтка, у́чится в университе́те на лингвисти́ческом факульте́те.

Карл, Герма́ния, Берли́н, бизнесме́н, комме́рческая фи́рма, студе́нт, университе́т, истори́ческий факульте́т

_____

_____

_____

Окса́на, Украи́на, Ки́ев, ме́неджер, магази́н, студе́нтка, ко́лледж, экономи́ческий факульте́т

_____

_____

_____

Лу́кас, Австра́лия, Ме́льбурн, юри́ст, юриди́ческая фи́рма, аспира́нт, университе́т, социологи́ческий факульте́т.

_____

_____

_____

Упражнéние 4.4. **Мой, твой, наш, ваш.** Describe the following items as "my", "your", "our":

Образéц: *моя* умная кошка

а) **Мой**, **моя́**, **моё** or **мои́**?

_____ *хороший друг* _____ *маленькая комната*

_____ *русские книги* _____ *смешное письмо*

б) **Твой**, **твоя́**, **твоё** or **твои́**?

_____ *дорогой компьютер* _____ *красивое платье*

_____ *интересная статья* _____ *новые друзья*

в) **Наш**, **на́ша**, **на́ше** or **на́ши**?

_____ *простое упражнение* _____ *трудный урок*

_____ *любимая песня* _____ *маленькие ошибки*

г) **Ваш**, **ва́ша**, **ва́ше** or **ва́ши**?

_____ *простые слова* _____ *новое общежитие*

_____ *английский словарь* _____ *старая квартира*

д) **Чей**, **чья**, **чьё** or **чьи**?

_____ *это рюкзак?* _____ *эта сумка?*

_____ *это радио?* _____ *это часы?*

Упражнéние 4.5. **О чём онú говорúли?** Insert the missing possessives in the prepositional case:

Образéц: *Преподаватель говорил о наших тестах.* (ours)

1. *Профессор говорил о _____ статье.* (my)

2. *Маша говорила о _____ друге.* (your, sing.)

3. *Они говорили о _____ студентах.* (your, pl. formal)

4. *О _____ работе вы говорили?* (whose)

5. *Мы говорили о _____ работе.* (your, sing. informal)

Упражнéние 4.6. **Что онú читáли?** Insert the missing possessives in the accusative case:

Образéц: *Студенты читали вашу книгу.* (your, pl. formal)

1. *Вы читали _____ перевод?* (my)

2. *Преподаватель читал _____ диалог.* (our)

3. *Она читала _____ письмо.* (your, sing. informal)

4. *Он читал _____ статью.* (your, pl. formal)

5. *Они читали _____ газету.* (our)

Упражнéние 4.7. **Перевóд. Personal pronouns in the accusative and prepositional cases.** Write the following questions and statements in Russian for your friend who wants to memorise them before his next Russian class.

1. — What is your name? *(formal)* _____

   — My name is Masha. _____

2. He often thinks about her. _____

3. She does not think about him. _____

4. She loves you. *(informal)* _____

5. I don't know him. _____

6. He knows you. _____

7. Do you know them?_____

8. They were talking about us. _____

 Упражне́ние 4.8. **Письмо́.** Read the letter from a Russian girl **Та́ня** and respond to it.

А) Письмо́ Тани́. Tanya's letter.

Здравствуйте, мои далёкие друзья!

Меня зовут Таня. Я живу в Иркутске. Это большой город на севере России. Я учусь в университете на лингвистическом факультете. Я изучаю русскую и английскую литературу, мировую историю, английский и немецкий языки. Учиться в университете не просто, поэтому я много занимаюсь. Обычно я занимаюсь дома: читаю, делаю домашнюю работу, слушаю английские и немецкие тексты и диалоги. Иногда я занимаюсь в библиотеке.

Я люблю слушать рок-музыку и американский джаз. А ещё я люблю читать. Мои любимые писатели — Лев Толстой, Владимир Набоков, Герман Гессе, Джон Толкин.

Расскажите о себе. Где вы живёте и учитесь? Что изучаете? В вашем университете трудно учиться? Вы много занимаетесь? Какую музыку вы любите слушать? Кто ваши любимые писатели?

Б) Ва́ше письмо́. Your letter. In your response letter, remember to answer Tanya's questions and use three study verbs: **изуча́ть**, **учи́ться**, **занима́ться**.

_____

_____

_____

_____

_____

_____

_____

_____

_____

_____

_____

_____

Повторя́ем. Chapter 4 Review

 Упражне́ние 4.9. **Что мы изуча́ли и что мы тепе́рь зна́ем.** Write a summary of what you have learned from chapter 4. You should mention:

Часть 1.

- what the topic was and what activities you did in class;
- what you talked about in class;
- what new verbs you learned and practiced (list three-four);
- what you learned about our characters Masha, Thomas, and Yumi

Часть 2.

- what new Russian words from this chapter are difficult to read (list four-six words)
- what new Russian words you do not remember well (list four-six words)
- what new Russian words you think are easy to read and remember (list three words)

You can refer to the text **Что мы изуча́ли** in Уро́к 7 (Те́ма 4) in your textbook, but do not copy it. Use the text in Уро́к 7 as a model to create your own.

Что мы изучали и что мы теперь знаем

Тема 4

Часть 1. _____

_____

_____

_____

_____

_____

_____

_____

_____

Часть 2. _____

_____

_____

_____

_____

_____

_____

_____

_____

_____

_____

Printed in Great Britain
by Amazon